CRICUT DESIGN SPACE FOR BEGINNERS

2020

A Step By Step Manual for New Users to Master the Cricut Design Space, Create Amazing Projects and Monetize their Skills

Lara Barron

© Copyright 2020, (Lara Barron)

All rights reserved.

The contents of this book may not be reproduced, duplicated or transmitted without direct written permission from the author. Under no circumstances will any legal responsibility or blame be held against the publisher for any reparation, damages, or monetary loss due to the information herein, either directly or indirectly.

Legal Notice:

This book is copyright protected. This is only for personal use. You cannot amend, distribute, sell, use, quote or paraphrase any part of the content within this book without the consent of the author

Table of Contents

INTRODUCTION 1
DIFFERENT CRICUT MODELS 4
   The Cricut Explore One....................... 4
   The Cricut Explore Air 5
   The Cricut Explore Air 2..................... 6
   The Cricut Maker 6
   The Cricut Joy 7
FUNCTION KEYS ON YOUR CRICUT MACHINE 10
CONFIGURATION OF CRICUT DESIGN SPACE.. 14
USING IMAGES IN CRICUT DESIGN SPACE 24
   Images Library 24
   Inserting Images 26
   CUTTING OUT AN IMAGE OUT OF ANOTHER IMAGE 27
   UPLOADING IMAGES ON THE CRICUT DESIGN SPACE................................. 28
EDITING PROJECTS ON DESIGN SPACE . 34

On Desktop/Laptop Version of Cricut Design Space 34

On App (iOS & Android) Version of Cricut Design Space 37

HOW TO USE CRICUT DESIGN SPACE ON YOUR IPAD 42

Top Panel 43

Canvas Area 44

Bottom Panel 45

GENERAL PROBLEMS OF THE CRICUT MACHINE AND SOLUTIONS 60

MAINTAINING YOUR CRICUT MACHINE .. 66

TIPS AND TRICKS TO BECOME A PRO CUTTER 69

BEST WAYS TO MAKE YOUR IDEAS COME ALIVE IN YOUR CRICUT PROJECTS 75

PURCHASING MATERIALS FOR YOUR CRICUT - SAVING COST 78

HOW TO START MAKING MONEY WITH YOUR CRICUT BUSINESS - SETTING THINGS UP 82

Setting up a website 82

Advertising 85

Taking Orders and Shipping 86
OTHER BOOKS BY THE AUTHOR 89
CONCLUSION.......................................90

INTRODUCTION

Welcome to the world of Cricut Design!

This book contains detailed, step by step instructions on how you can master the Cricut Design Space. You will also learn how to manage your Cricut Design Space on your Desktop, iOS (iPad) and Android device. Moreover, this manual will teach you how to move your files within these three work spaces (Desktop, Android and iOS.) You will also learn how to make your own unique ideas into awesome Cricut projects that will earn you money and set you on a journey to mastery.

Filled with screenshots and easy-to-understand steps, this book is the perfect beginner's manual. There are various lessons you will learn from this book and you will be equipped with the necessary skills to create beautiful designs and how to monetize your designs to earn money, check out the table of content for the many topics that will be covered in this book.

You don't need to have a prior knowledge of Cricut before you can use this book, this manual contains everything you need to know and much more.

What are you then waiting for? Read on!

DIFFERENT CRICUT MODELS

Hi there! Have you heard of Cricut? Possibly. However, do you know that there are various machines manufactured to meet your cutting taste? Here, check them out.

The Cricut Explore One

This machine right here is the most basic and dare I say, relatively the cheapest of the Cricut cutting machines. It has the ability to cut, write and score a wide range of materials and does not require cartridges. The downside to it is that, it is not Bluetooth enabled and you cannot do two activities at the same time. One has to come before the other, that is write then cut, or score before cutting.

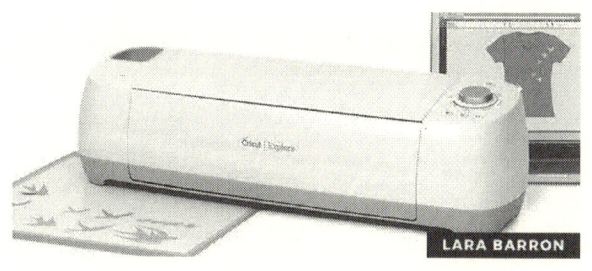

The Cricut Explore Air

When you hear of an upgrade, this is one. The Cricut Explore Air comes as a plus as it is Bluetooth-enabled so you can by-pass your USB cord and what's more, you can carry out two functions at the same time. With the secondary tool holder, you can write and cut or score and cut simultaneously.

The Cricut Explore Air 2

Don't get confused, it is a just one of the machines in the Cricut Explore line. However, are you looking for a machine that cuts twice as fast as the previous machines and a few more materials, then you've just ended your search with the Cricut Explore Air 2. More so, it comes in a variety of colours just to add some spice.

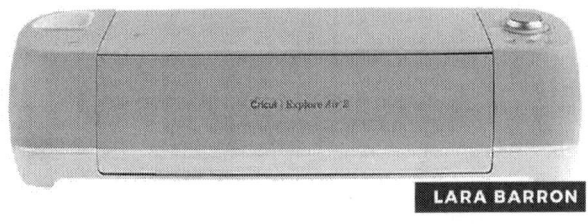
LARA BARRON

The Cricut Maker

This machine is the Cricut Explore and more. What's more? Using the Rotary Blade, the Cricut Maker can cut unbounded fabric unlike the other lines of machines that require a stabiliser. It can also score all sorts of materials using a tool that is an upgrade to the Scoring Stylus, the Scoring Wheel. It cuts thicker materials and has more tools such as the engraving tool, the wavy rotary tool, the perforation tool and the debossing tool.

LARA BARRON

The Cricut Joy

Recently unveiled is the Cricut Joy and it is worth the joy that comes with it. It is a surprisingly smaller machine, less than half the size of its predecessors and its new features include mat-free cutting. This means you can cut up to 20' feet of Vinyl at a go. Isn't that just lovely? It also comes with a Card Mat which can come in handy for making various types of cards.

It however comes with a single blade and a pen holder. If you want to get a Cricut machine without spending too much, you can go for the Cricut Joy machine.

LARA BARRON

You possibly might have heard of other models of the Cricut Cutting Machine but they were the first generational machines that were manufactured and are actually out-dated.

FUNCTION KEYS ON YOUR CRICUT MACHINE

Now that you've got your machine, those buttons might be catching your attention. The buttons on the Cricut Maker are under the top lid while that of the Explore series are at the right of the machine on display. There are:

•**The Open button**: this is located on the left side of the Cricut machine though it isn't seen in the Cricut Maker and Joy. Once you press this button, the doors of your machine (Cricut Explore series) open slowly.

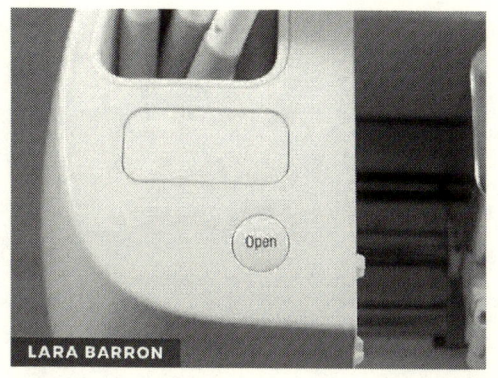

•**The Power Button:** situated at the right side of your machine. It is for switching the machine on or off. When it is connected to Bluetooth, the light is blue and if it is connected via USB cord, it is white in colour.

•**The Smart dial:** is also only available in the Explore series and is select the kind of material you are working with. Although custom materials will have to be selected on the Cricut Design Space. It is located at the middle of the right side of the machine.

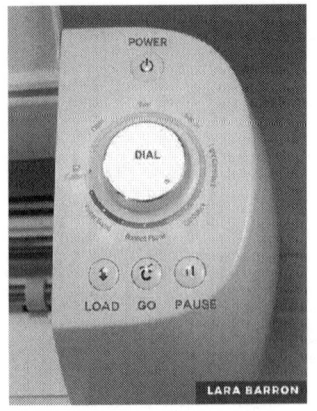 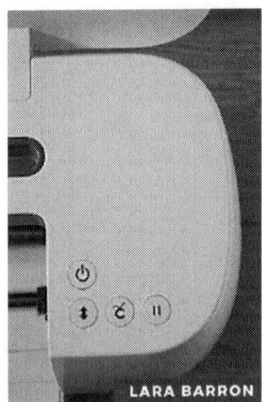

- **The Load button:** this is the first of the last row of buttons you'll see on the right side of the Cricut machine. It is used to load/unload a mat before and after cutting/printing a project.

- **Cut/Go button:** this button bears the Cricut logo on it and it is used to start cutting when a mat with a material has been loaded into the machine.

- **Pause button:** the last of the bottom row of buttons on the left side of the Cricut machine basically to pause cutting.

CONFIGURATION OF CRICUT DESIGN SPACE

You cannot work with any of your Cricut machines without the Design Space App and to make the maximum use of its features, you'll have to set or change some settings. And here's how to go about it:

1. Preliminary Warm-up:

I call this warm-up because all you need to do is to plug in the machine and power it on. Then pair your machine with your desktop or device via Bluetooth or connect via USB cord.

2. Download the App:

If you're using a PC or laptop, just type in https://design.cricut.com on your web browser and get directed to sign in or create your Cricut ID. If you will be working with your iOS device such as your iPhone or iPad, visit the App store and type in "Cricut Design Space" in the search box. For Android devices, go to the Play Store and you can download it by searching on "Cricut Design Space". After the download, launch the app and either sign in or create a Cricut ID.

Android PlayStore

iOS App Store

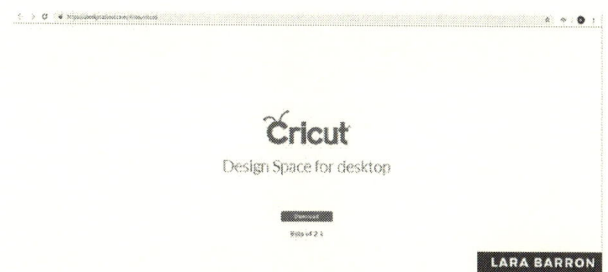

Desktop Version

3. Setup your machine:

For iOS and Android devices, tap on the Menu and select Machine Setup & App Overview. Tap on New Machine Setup and from there, all you need to do is to follow the on-screen instructions till you are asked to make your first project.

Home

Canvas

New Machine Setup

Calibration

Manage Custom Materials

Update Firmware

Account Details

Link Cartridges

Cricut Access

Settings

Legal

New Features

United States ▼

Help

Sign Out

LARA BARRON

iOS/Android App

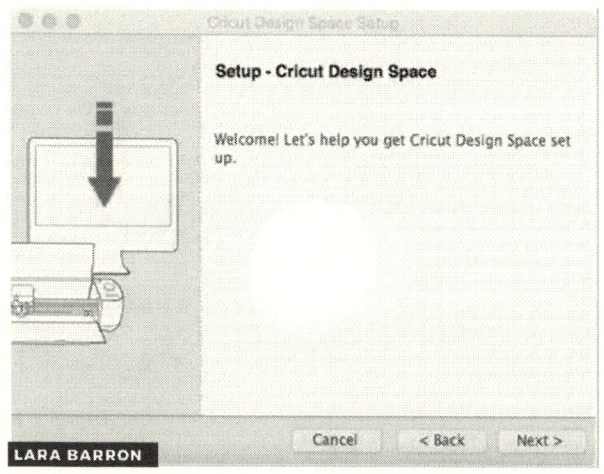

Desktop Version

4. Work on the Grid Settings:

Once you are done downloading and installing the App, and setting up your machine, it brings up a large space for designs called the Canvas. This canvas has a full grid by default that it can be a bother working with it. Good thing is that you can change its measurements and how it appears on your screen.

On your desktop or laptop, click on the blank space between the zeros in the top left corner of your rulers to remove the grid lines while you can go to the three lines menu in the upper left corner, pick on Settings and then choose whatever parameters in inches or centimetres.

Meanwhile, for iOS and Android devices, go to settings in the bottom toolbar and tap on toggle Grids to remove the grid lines or tap on toggle Metric Units on or off to change the grid's measurements.

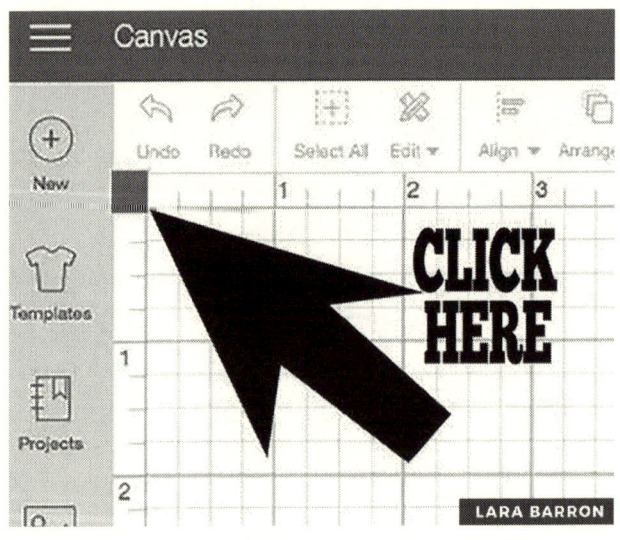

5. Turn On/Off the Smart Guides:

These Smart Guides are a feature of the Cricut Design Space app on iOS and Android devices and are to help position things on the Canvas in relation to others. But they may constitute a nuisance by giving you issues with positioning things on your Canvas. To switch off the Smart Guides, tap Settings in the bottom toolbar and turn SmartGuides off.

With the above, then you are ready to have a glimpse of the world of creativity.

Canvas Settings

Metric Units

Grids

Smart Guides
Helps align and position objects relative to other items on the canvas.

Settings

LARA BARRON

USING IMAGES IN CRICUT DESIGN SPACE

Images Library

To find, add or insert images on the design space, there is the Images Icon. A click on this Images Icon produces a screen of the Image Library. This library is classified into images, categories and cartridges. On the screen to the topmost right, there is the search bar just to the topmost right with the filters button next to it.

This search and filters tools in the image library help to narrow the display of images according to what you desire. For example, if you search for cars, only images with or related to cars will be displayed on the screen for ease and time management. A filter makes your search easy to sort by ownership, type or layers. Ownership of images could be through the fact that the images were predesigned on your free machine software, was uploaded by you, through membership that is, Cricut Access or by purchase. The Type subheading has options ranging from cards, envelops, printables, etc. and the Layer subheading suggesting either single or multiple layers.

Filters could be combined thus making your search narrower and more specific. For example, clicking on Cricut Access, cards and multiple layers on the drop-down, it would show only images from Cricut Access that have such features. Combining these two tools drastically reduces the number of search replies and saves your time.

Once the images are loaded, there are ways of identifying them. At the bottom of each image, you'll either see a price or words like Free, Subscribed or Purchased. At the right side of the bottom, there's an information icon which reveals more about the image. You'll get specifics like the image name, ID number, the Cartridge name and the option to buy the image. You can get more images from that cartridge by clicking on the cartridge name which automatically switches your search from the Images classification on the bar to Cartridges. If the image has a green cricut icon at the topmost left, it means the image is available on the Cricut Access.

Inserting Images

After a search for whatever image you desire for your project, click on the most suitable image. Once it gets highlighted and shows to the right bottom of the screen that it is queued, you can go on to click on the Insert image button that is placed right next to it. The image is then inserted on the canvas.

You can also select multiple images by highlighting more than one image depending on what you want. You can also deselect an image if you do not want to add it anymore or click on the red button on the image when it is already on the canvas. When the images show up on the canvas, you can then go on to edit or work on them either individually or as a layer.

CUTTING OUT AN IMAGE OUT OF ANOTHER IMAGE

One major tool comes to play when cutting an image out of another image and that is the Slice tool. It splits two overlapping images or texts into different parts by creating cut paths. Note the following however:

• You can use the Slice tool to cut shape or text from another shape or cut overlapping shapes out.

• With images, Slice works with only two layers at a time.

• If the images have more than two layers, you can hide or ungroup other layers to use the Slice tool.

Steps in cutting out images from another image include:

1. Arrange the images in such a way that they overlap.

2. Select/ highlight both the images.

3. Click on the Slice icon at the bottom of the Layers Panel. The images will reflect in the Layer Panel as sliced images.

4. Separate the layers, edit or delete the images independently.

UPLOADING IMAGES ON THE CRICUT DESIGN SPACE

To upload images on Cricut Design Space, there is the Upload Icon on the Design Panel. Images can be uploaded once you create them or purchase them. On clicking the Upload button, the images are automatically detected by the Design Space either as a Basic or Vector Image.

There are a few differences between these kinds of images. A basic image is made up of different individual coloured squares arranged together to form a complete picture. Basic images are pictures files with .jpg, .gif, .png, .bmp. Their advantages include them having features like smooth gradients and subtle tones. They are also great options for pattern uploads and print-then-cut projects. One disadvantage is that they cannot be scaled up as they would lose picture quality, hence they can only be effectively scaled down. Also, they are relatively larger files and require more technical efforts to be converted to cut files.

Vector Images, used in (graphics design software) on the other hand aren't all that rudimentary as they follow mathematical paths. They have file extensions of .svg and .dxf (these are the only two compatible with Cricut Design Space). They can be uploaded with little to no need of editing plus no loss of picture quality when you scale them up. In addition, they are typically smaller files when compared to basic images. However for projects, they mostly require colour and size changes.

To upload Vector images:

i. Clicking the Upload Icon, a page appears with options.
ii. Click on the Upload Image button.
iii. Next, you either drag and drop or use the browse for image option.
iv. For the browse method, you find the image and click on it.
v. Name and tag the image giving whatever name or description makes it easy for you to find the image the next time you might need it.
vi. Once you are done naming, you may click the save option and your image is ready for use either at the moment or later.

To upload Basic Images:

i. Click on the Upload Icon, a page appears with options.
ii. Click on the Upload Image button.
iii. Once you have selected the image, you need to select the image type as simple, moderately complex or complex. This can be determined by the number of shapes, colours, contrast and details.
iv. Once the Image Type is selected, click on Continue to progress.
v. The picture is placed on the Canvas with the magic wand, eraser and crop tools at the topmost left of the Screen just beneath the Header. To the topmost right are the Undo, Redo and Zoom commands. Advanced options button is also available at the left side on the Screen. At the bottom, there are the Back, Preview, Cancel and Continue buttons.

vi. Once you are done editing, you can then save the image as Cut or Print-then-Cut Image. Note that images with complex colours are better saved as Print-then-Cut images.
vii. Name and tag the image for easy identification in the Image Library.
viii. Click Save and your image is ready for use.

To learn how to create up to 50 interesting, unique Cricut designs with screenshots to guide you, check out the book I wrote on that on Amazon. Reading that book will give additional skills to become a world class Pro in Cricut design. You can find the link to the Paperback and E-book copy in the "OTHER BOOKS BY THE AUTHOR" section.

EDITING PROJECTS ON DESIGN SPACE

So, you've got some saved works or designs on design space and you want to edit them, how do you go about it? The following are tips and tricks in editing projects in Cricut Design Space:

On Desktop/Laptop Version of Cricut Design Space

Definitely, you must have saved the project you want to edit previously. So, the first thing to note in order to open previously saved project is that you will need a new canvas. So here goes:

1. Get your design(s):

This can be done by clicking on the My Projects shortcut at the right-hand corner of the screen. Another route you may want to take is by clicking on the 'My Projects' option on the left panel of the

Canvas and select 'My Projects' on the drop-down.

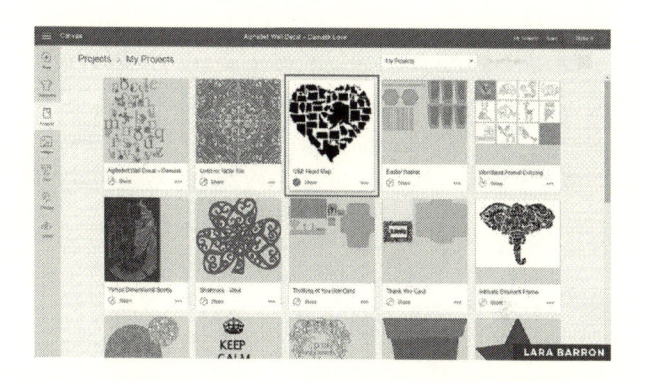

2. Use the 'Customise'/Edit option:

Once you find the desired design, click on it. A small window appears with different options and at this point, you are only concerned with the 'Customise/Edit' option. This option once clicked on, enables you to edit your designs and make changes to them.

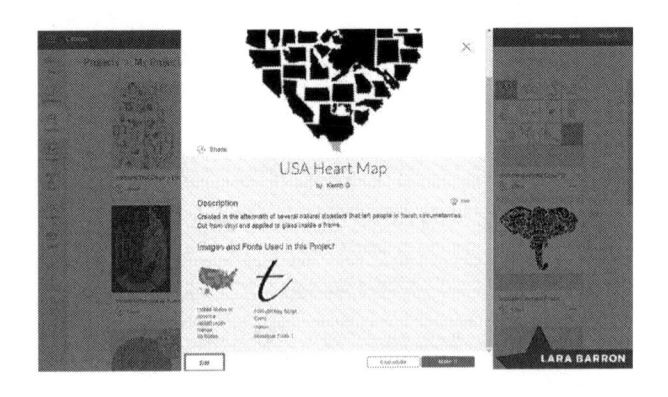

3. Edit your design:

At this point, you can add or change the fonts, add or change shape, weld, slice or attach images to the borders of your creativity. It all depends on what you want.

4. Save or Save As:

If you are interested in keeping both the original and edited designs, click on 'Save' and pick on the 'Save As' option. This way you are allowed to name the edited version differently in order to save both designs. However, if you are only interested in having the edited design only, clicking on the Save option makes you override the original design.

On App (iOS & Android) Version of Cricut Design Space

This is quite different from its desktop version in that the app version has three views. These views are Home, Canvas and Make. To edit designs, follow these steps:

1. Fetch your designs:

To open a previously crated and saved project, you will have to have a clean canvas. Once that is ensured, tap on the 'Home' view of the Design Space app. This view has a drop-down just below your profile picture where you can click on. Select where your Project is saved to (Cloud or iPad/iPhone).

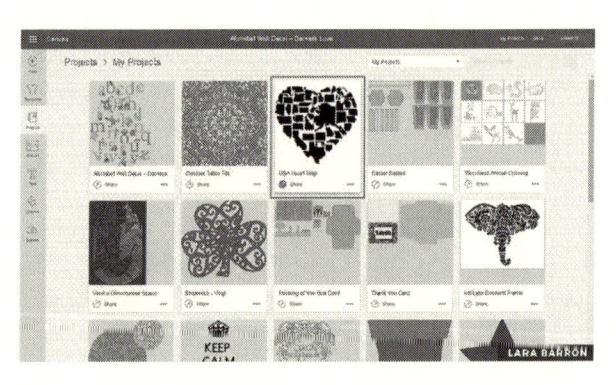

2. Use the 'Customise'/Edit option:

Once you find the desired design, click on it. A small window appears with different options and at this point, you are only concerned with the 'Customise/Edit' option. This option once clicked on, enables you to edit your designs and make changes to them.

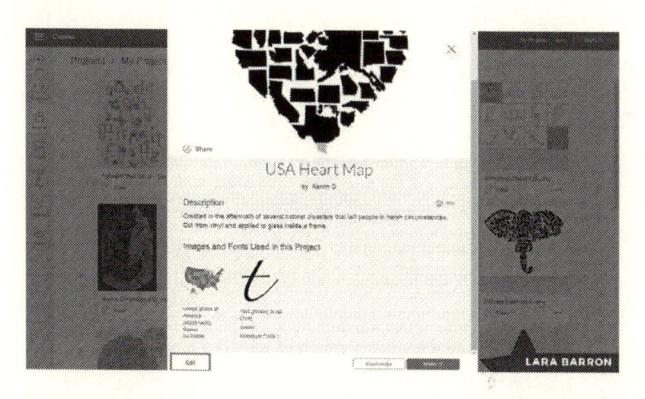

3. Edit your design:

At this point, you can add or change the fonts, add or change shape, weld, slice or attach images to the borders of your creativity. It all depends on what you want.

4. Save or Save As:

If you are interested in keeping both the original and edited designs, click on 'Save' and pick on the 'Save As' option. This way you are allowed to name the edited version differently in order to save both designs. However, if you are only interested in having the edited design only, clicking on the Save option makes you override the original design.

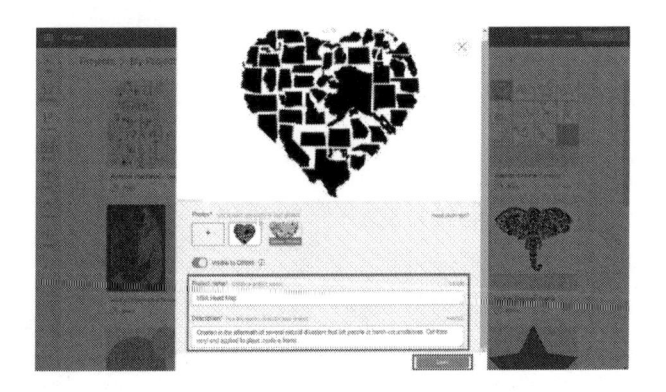

HOW TO USE CRICUT DESIGN SPACE ON YOUR IPAD

The iPad app version of the Cricut Design Space is very easy to navigate and use once you know its rules and while many might be used to the desktop/laptop version, the iPad is just a very portable device that makes creating designs easier and location-friendly. Creativity just went beyond the borders.

On the Top Panel, the iPad has the Home, Canvas and Make views but on opening the App, you will be in the Home section. This view enables you to pick one of a ready to cut project, images or Create a New Project. The Canvas view comes on when you tap on 'New Project' and to really know how to work your way through creating and cutting, you might have to understand the various panels and icons there is, on the Design Space.

Top Panel

On this panel, there are a range of icons that permits you to access your profile, projects and the Canvas.

i. Profile Picture-Settings: Tapping on your profile picture opens up a menu with a variety of settings options such as Machine Selection, Machine Setup and App Overview among others.
ii. Save: this option only gets activated when you have a character or shape on the Canvas.
iii. Home/Canvas/Make: these buttons stand for the different view that there is and a darker shade on any of the buttons shows what view you are on.

• Home is a button for beginnings. It is essential if. you want to start all over or add something new.

• Canvas is the area where designs are made/created before cutting.

- Make is the option to tap when you are completed with your projects and ready to proceed to cutting. To get there, there is the 'Make it' button on the Bottom Panel, tap it and move here.

iv. Expand: this option makes the Canvas area larger while making other menus disappear so that you can see and assess your designs with more ease. Tap on the same option again to return to standard view.

Canvas Area

This area is the playing ground where you get down with designs, try, create and perfect your projects before cutting them.

i. Measurements: Remember grids? Well, while they are often turned off, they divide the canvas area and help you work hand in hand with the cutting mat when designing.

ii. Selection: when you select one or more layers, they are highlighted in blue colour but different action scan be carried out via the four corners. The red X represents Delete. The right upper corner allows you to rotate the image. The tiny lock allows you to keep the side proportional when using the lower right button to either increase or decrease the size of the layer. Between the lock and the lower right button, a fifth option can be initiated. It is useful in creating a 3D perspective to your design by tapping on it and dragging your design.

Bottom Panel

This panel pools most of the options that would have otherwise be shared into different panels on the desktop/laptop version into one place at the bottom.

Options here include the Image, Text, Shapes, Upload, Actions, Edit, Sync, Layers, Undo, Redo, Camera, Settings, and Make It options. Once you tap on any of the options, that icon turns green on the grey bottom panel.

i. Add Image: most projects will be incomplete without images. Most often than not, we express our creativity with a combo of images alongside other characters/elements. Images can be sought for using keywords, categories or cartridges, and can fetched from previously uploaded images on your device/cloud.

A click on this Images Icon produces a screen of the Image Library. This library is classified into images, categories and cartridges. 'Cartridges' is particularly a library for images that need to be purchased though a few come with subscription on Cricut Access.

ii. Add Text: this icon comes in handy when you wish to add some lettering to your projects and as such, you have the luxury of working with various fonts either from Cricut or your device. Once this icon is tapped on, you will be prompted to choose what font you want to work with, and a text box appears on your Canvas for you to type in.

iii. Add Shapes: these shapes ensure you have simple and yet, elegant projects.

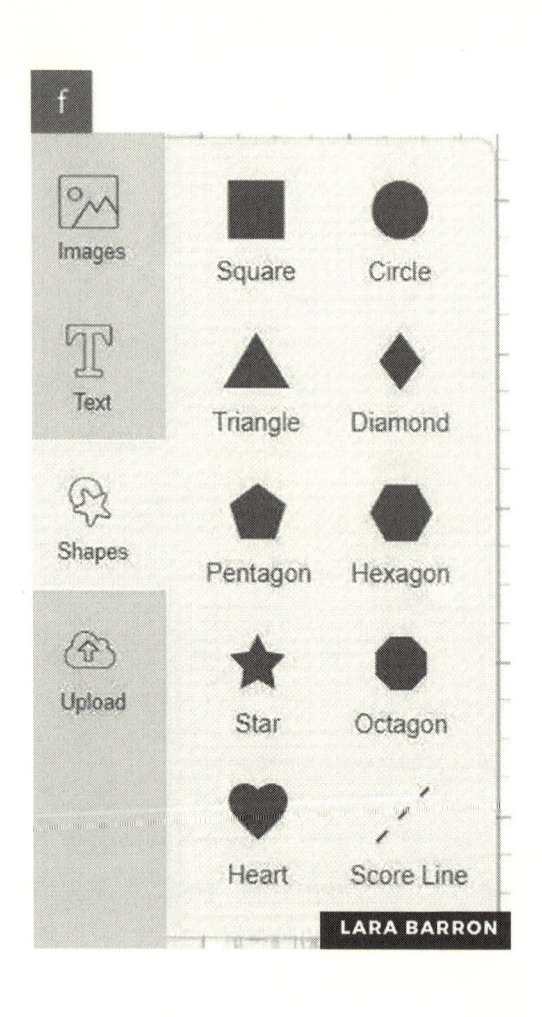

iv. Upload: this option enables you to upload files and images you want to cut to whatever location you intend to.

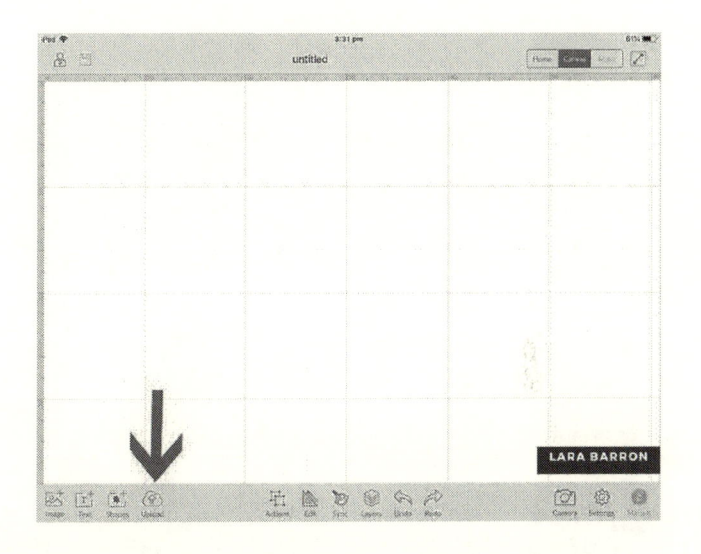

v. Actions: are you thinking of changing or redefining your design? Then this option has a lot of features for that. Here they are:

• Group: this icon groups texts, images and layers together so that they can be sized and moved together on the Canvas.

• Ungroup: the letters in text still get grouped together, however this icon ungroups sets of layers, images or texts so that they can be edited separately on the Canvas.

• Slice: used for cutting shapes, text, and separating layers when working projects.

• Weld: creates one object from multiple layers without any demarcating lines showing or combining different elements into one.

• Attach: ensures that objects on the mat are exactly as the objects appearing on the Canvas.

• Detach: separates previously attached layers back into their individual layers once again.

• Flatten: unites several layers into one to become one printable image, thus acts as an extra support for Print and Cut actions.

• Unflatten: splits merged layers from an image into individual layers.

- Duplicate: produces copies of the same object on the Canvas.

- Isolate Letters: this option on the App version is for text layers. It enables you to be able to edit each letter singly.

- Contour: this icon acts as a hide/show icon and allows you to hide unwanted pieces from a design. It also allows you to cut lines/sketches on a layer.

vi. Edit Menu: this permits further editing of text on Layers Panel. Features under this menu include:

- Font: if you are looking for fonts to work with when designing, just tap on this option. If you are subscribed to Cricut Access, there are Cricut fonts you can use alongside your System fonts. Otherwise, you can purchase them.

- Style: this option gives you a chance to add a twist to your creativity. You can change the style of your fonts. It could be regular, bold, italic, bold italic or writing style.

• Alignment (for text only): this helps organise your text of words and sentences into lines and paragraphs. It has three sub-options: Left, Centre and Right all depending on how and where you want your paragraph to be aligned to.

• Size, Letter and Line Space: with this amazing feature, you can increase or reduce the size of your fonts, determine the space between fonts/letters as well as control the spacing between lines.

• Line Type and Fill: this is like a manual for your machine. It tells your machine what you want it to do. There are the following options to pick from: Cut, Draw, Score, Engrave, Deboss, Wave, and Perf.

However, depending on what machine you are dealing with, these options may and may not be totally available. A Cricut Explore machine will only enable you gain access to the Cut, Draw and Score options while a Cricut Maker has all the options available for use.

The Fill in this feature only works when you are using the Cut option and is mainly for printing so if you will not be printing, you have the No Fill to tap on. If you will be cutting after your designs are out on your materials, then you've got the Print option.

• Size: looking for a way to size a project into the exact measurements you have in mind, no worries 'cause this option got you.

• Rotate: you can place or position any design or project into an angle or a certain degree you want with this 'Rotate' option.

• Flip: have you been wishing you can have a reflected image of a particular design? Then this option is all you need plus it has some side dishes to it. They are Flip Horizontal and Flip Vertical.

• Position: this makes you determine the position of the object on the Canvas either by typing in the desired distance from the top left corner of the canvas or adjusting it by 0.1 at a time.

• Arrange: organises or changes how objects are placed on the canvas and provides the following functions: Sent to Back, Move Backward, Move Forward and Sent to Front.

Arrange

Send To Back

Move Backward

Move Forward

Send To Front

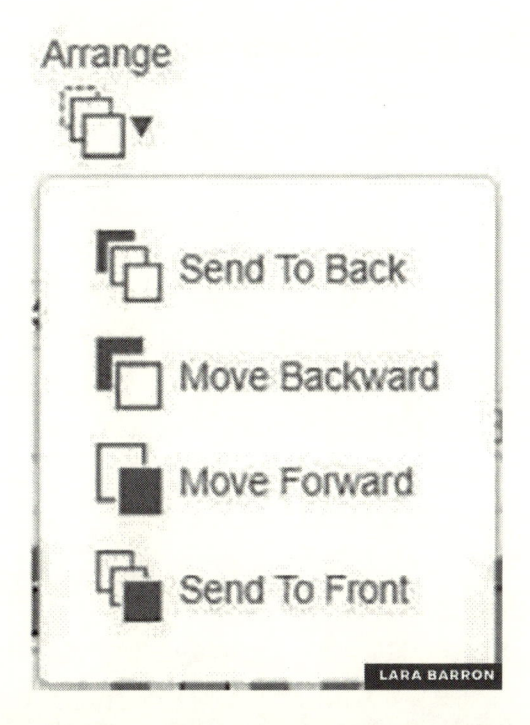

- Alignment: This comes in handy when you wish to adjust two or more objects either to the margins, centre or spatially using the following options: Center, Align Left, Align Center, Align Right, Align Top, Align Middle, and Align Bottom.

- Distribute: this helps with ensuring the same spacing between characters or elements on your design. However, note that for this option to be activated, you must have at least three characters/elements highlighted. This distribution can be made 'Horizontally' or 'Vertically'.

vii. Sync: your design probably has different colours or different shades of the same colour and you aren't cool with it? Just tap the shade of colour you want out of the picture and drag it dropping it on the shade you want to work with. That way, you can have just a colour for the whole design or project.

viii. Layers: tapping on this icon ushers in a panel at the right side of the Canvas and it provides you with these options:

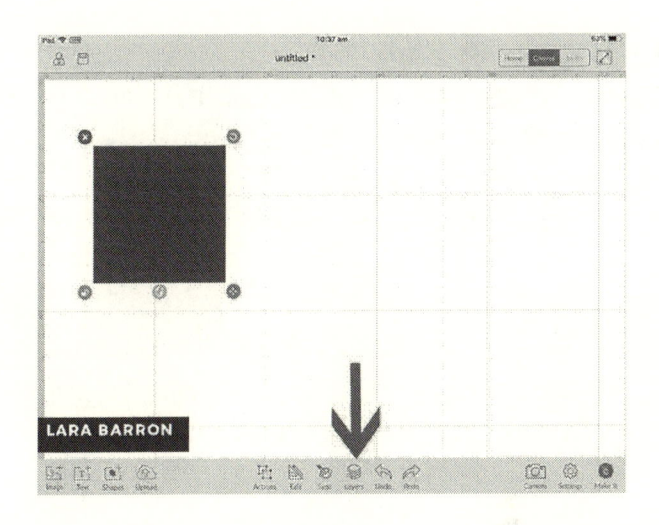

• Duplicate: this option duplicates any layer or design you have selected on the Layers panel or Canvas.

• Layer Visibility: There are times you are not sure if you should delete an element from a design or change its position. This option can then be used to hide such an element so you can reach a very beautiful conclusion. This helpful option is represented by the eye symbol on the Layers panel which shows up a cross mark when an element is hidden.

- Delete: all you need to do to use this option is to highlight/select the elements you want deleted and tap on it.

ix. Undo-Redo: this option can be used when a mistake is made and you want to correct it. The 'Redo' option can be used to rectify an action that you made in error, for example, restoring a deleted element.

x. Camera: Unlike what you know about camera options, this serves as a visual aid before cutting. This means you are able to have a clear picture of your completed design before cutting.

xi. Settings: this enables to choose whether or not you want Metric Units, Grid lines and Smart Guides turned on or off.

xii. Make It: the icon you tap on once you've made and perfected your design and it's ready to be cut or printed.

xiii. Project Copies: located at the upper left corner of your iPad, this icon is used if you want to cut more than one project.
xiv. Snap Mat: this icon located at the bottom left corner enables you to visualise and then choose the exact place you want to cut your designs. Tapping on this icon automatically activates the camera.
xv. Continue: Once you are sure everything is set and you are ready to cut, tap on the 'Continue' icon and you will be led to another set of instructions for the best cut.

GENERAL PROBLEMS OF THE CRICUT MACHINE AND SOLUTIONS

1. Blade not being detected in Cricut Maker: you may do the following moving to the next step if the problem still persists after a previous intervention.

• Ensure that the tool installed in Clamp b matches the tool recommended by design Space in the Load tools step on the project preview screen. If it is not the rccommended tool, you may unload the mat to return to the project preview screen and the, select the Edit Tools link to choose a different tool.

• Remove the tool from Clamp B and press the flashing Go button.

• Remove the tool from Clamp B. Gently clean the tool sensor with compressed air or a microfiber cloth. Reinstall the tool in Clamp B and press the flashing Go button.

• Attempt a test project with a basic shape using a different adaptive system tool such as the Knife Blade, Scoring Wheel or Rotary Blade.

• Uninstall the Design Space app. Restart the computer and reboot the Cricut Maker machine. Reinstall the Design Space app and attempt the project again. If the problem still persists, contact the Member Care.

2. My machine is making an unusual noise: this could be grinding or loud in nature.

If it is a Grinding Noise:

• Make a brief video of the issue and contact Member Care if it is from the carriage car when you push the cut button.

- Also contact Member Care if it is a new machine and the noise starts from its first use.

- Ensure you are using the power cord that came with the machine as the unusual noise may be from the wrong voltage from another cord.

- Ensure you are using the adequate pressure for whatever material you are cutting. The noise might be due to high pressure settings. You can reduce the pressure by clicking on 'Edit Custom Materials' from the upper right of the cut preview after clicking 'Change Material' and try reducing the pressure settings.

If it is a Loud Noise:

- The Fast Mode might be the reason for such but if it is not in use, make a video with the noise and contact the Member Care.

3. My machine is tearing or dragging through my material:

• Make sure you have selected the correct material setting in Design Space or that the Smart Dial is on the correct setting or the proper material is selected from the Custom drop-down menu.

• Verify the size and intricacy of the image. If it is a very intricate and small image, try cutting a simpler and larger one. If this addresses the issue, then try cutting intricate images using the Custom setting for Cardstock-Intricate Cuts. If the machine is on Fast Mode, turn it off and attempt to cut again.

• Remove the blade housing from the machine, them, remove the blade and check for any debris inside the housing or on the blade.

• Reduce the pressure settings for that material type in the Mange Custom Materials screen by increments of 2-4. This may need to be done 2-3 times to change the cut result.

• Attempt cutting a different material to check if the problem is with the material you are trying to cut.

• Try using a new blade and/or mat.

• You may contact the Member Care if the issue still persists.

4. My Cricut machine keeps turning off in the middle of my cut:

• If you are working with foil or metal sheets, it may be due to Static Electricity build-up which can be initiated or worsened by dry environments. So, use a spray bottle with water to spray a mist into the air to dissipate the build-up or use a humidifier/vaporizer.

If you have other problems with any of your Cricut Machines, you can log in to Cricut help centre at https://help.cricut.com. There, you can also get contact details of the Member Care.

MAINTAINING YOUR CRICUT MACHINE

Here's how to ensure your machine works efficiently for a longer period of time:

1. Place your machine on a firm, flat surface with a lot of airy space around it. It must be kept in a dry, clean area.

2. Ensure that all connections are secure if in use and gently plugged out after use. Also ensure the proper cord and the right amount of voltage.

3. Ensure clean surfaces and ports of the machine. It is advisable to clean with oil-free wipes. For rails, wheels, cutting heads, bar and rollers, you can use an alcohol swab ensuring there are no debris, pieces of cut materials, grease etc.

4. Take good care of your blades. Clean out debris from blade holder and replace dull or broken blades.

5. Do not cut in areas where dust, excess humidity or moisture can cause damage to machine components.

6. Replace all old and worn out materials such as mats, strips, tapes, etc.

7. Use the right pressure for specific cutting materials.

TIPS AND TRICKS TO BECOME A PRO CUTTER

Follow these simple steps and put an end to your times of struggling:

1. Keep your Cutting Mats covers: keeps your mats clean and free from dust. That way, you are free from cut interferences.

2. Always have good tools: they come in handy when you need them for trimming, weeding, and so on. Invest in tools that will last for a long time and not those that will have faults on your second usage.

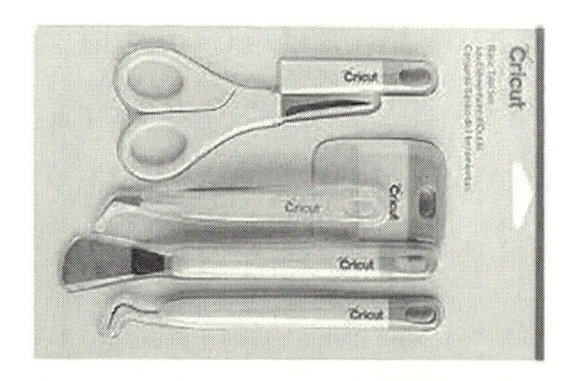

3. Always have extra blades handy: blades are bound to become dull after a period of use. For better and cleaner cuts, a new and sharp blade should be available.

LARA BARRON

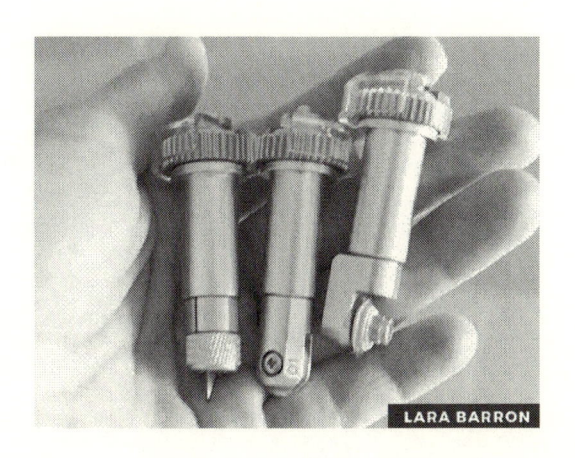

4. Always Mirror Iron-on Images: most often than not, he shiny part of your vinyl is placed on cloth side of the material you are using, thus giving a back picture of your image which doesn't point you out as a pro. So mirror your images and you have them, coming out better and in the right way.

5. Use gravity to peel your projects off the mats: This prevents your paper coming out all curled-up.

6. Get a Cricut EasyPress: Bring on your cutting game with the Cricut EasyPress, ironing vinyl and making customised clothing haven't been any easier and efficient.

7. Use more pressure: more pressure makes weeding easier and makes your cutting better.

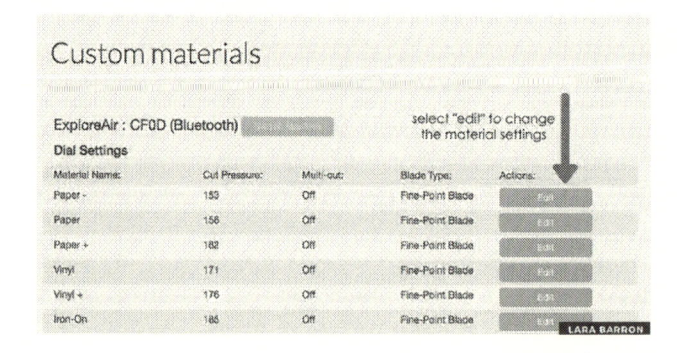

BEST WAYS TO MAKE YOUR IDEAS COME ALIVE IN YOUR CRICUT PROJECTS

Ever tried to kindle a flame for your ideas to sparkle? Try these:

1. Practice with different materials.

2. Don't underestimate your creativity.

3. Explore with different elements on Design Space.

4. Watch variety of tutorials online on Cricut crafts.

5. Make judicious use of the Edit options.

6. Hang out with friend and make cutting part of your activities.

7 You weren't so perfect the previous time? Try again and don't give up!

PURCHASING MATERIALS FOR YOUR CRICUT - SAVING COST

Are you new to Cricut cutting machines and while buying supplies, you want to save cost? Follow these pieces of advice:

1 Buy Cutting mats but don't forget Spray Adhesive:

Cricut cutting mats come in colours, each for a different range of materials. While it might quickly lose its stickiness due to use, it is not impossible to reuse mats. So instead of buying over and over again, you can clean used ones and use the spray adhesive to make them sticky again.

2 Cricut pens are fine but get a pen adapter as well:

These pens come in handy when you are working with cards and labels but can be expensive as well. A pen adapter works very well with your machine but what's more? It allows you to use any other kind of pen or marker- other than the Cricut pens. There you go, saving some cash.

3 Order in Bulk:

Are you ready to get your supplies? Why not get them in bulk probably with some other friends and you can keep the extra change. It's worth it, you know?

4 Work with free files and fonts:

Probably, you are still saving up money for other materials, you can make do with free designs and fonts on the Design Space.

5 Go for appliances that don't consume much:

You definitely already have appliances that consume energy and I'm sure you are not planning to add to your bills. So, I'll recommend Cricut EasyPress as a heat press - it gives you a commendable iron-on service and is power-friendly.

Gotten your Cricut machine and your supplies? Got a device you are ready to work with? Welcome to the world of crafting with Cricut.

HOW TO START MAKING MONEY WITH YOUR CRICUT BUSINESS - SETTING THINGS UP

Setting up a website

This is a very important step in the right direction and here's how you can go about it:

1. Choose a domain name/URL

This is very important because this is what your audience or customers will know you by and everything you create and post will be linked to this domain name. Usually, you can pick one that depicts your brand and what you do. It must be short and easy to remember also.

2. Register your domain name/URL

This can be done with little cash, usually per annum and its helps link your domain name to your hosting service. I would recommend using godaddy for domain and hosting services.

3. Choosing a hosting service

You will need a hosting service to host your website and depending on their customer service, reliability, speed, storage space among others, you can choose one that is very good.

4. Connect your domain name to your web host

Some web host will not need this step as they offer domain names with their hosting service. However, for those that don't, you will have to connect your domain name by plugging your server name/DNS into your domain name registrar account.

5. Install WordPress

WordPress is an application that allows you to manage and work on your website and it is absolutely free, straight forward and consumer friendly.

6. Choose a theme for your website

Get one that suits your brand, content and services. You can get them free or subscribe for Premium ones at a price.

7. Configure your website

Now that you've got a functional website with a theme to it, you may want to configure your website. You will want to organise the information you give about what you do and what you have to offer, add one or more colours and make it easy for visitors to navigate through your site.

8. Add content

Get all yourself out there by uploading, writing and posting what you have to offer on your website. Something that will appeal to your customers and leave them satisfied.

If setting up your website is something you know you may not be able to do on your own, you can employ the service of a web developer to create your website. This will help you focus on making money with your Cricut by creating more designs.

Advertising

Common ways of advertising as a new service provider include:

• Social media ads on Instagram, Pinterest, Facebook and other social media sites.

- Video Ads on blogs, YouTube, etc.

- Digital display ads

- Magazines and newspapers

- Direct mail and personal sales

Other means are:

- Outdoor Advertising

- Radio and Podcasts

- Product Placement on Television shows and YouTube channels.

- Email marketing.

- Event marketing.

Taking Orders and Shipping

Customers can place orders via email or contact phone numbers that you place on your website. It could be daily or within specified time limits or days depending on how well you can deliver. Ensure you get all necessary arrangements in place before taking orders from areas far from your reach so as to prevent disappointments and delays thus, ruining your reputation as a service provider.

Shipping arrangements depend on your location and the taxes involved.

Saving money using your Cricut Explore machine for business

You can employ the services of any bank or saving institutions around you to build your financial strength as well as grow your wealth.

NOTE:

i.   If you took a loan, ensure you pay off your debt.

ii.   On your first batch of sales, take out your capital to continue business and save the profit.

OTHER BOOKS BY THE AUTHOR

CRICUT EXPLORE AIR 2 FOR BEGINNERS: The Ultimate Guide to Master the Cricut Explore Air 2, with Original Projects and How to Monetize your Ideas and Designs by LARA BARRON.

Paperback Link:
https://www.amazon.com/dp/1656185148

E-book Link:
https://www.amazon.com/dp/B084LQGHN3

CONCLUSION

Thank you again for purchasing this book filled with simple and direct lessons!

It is my hope that you have been able to familiarize yourself with the Cricut Design Space through the different lessons in this book. By applying the steps in this book, you will be able to create amazing Cricut projects for yourself, friends and your family. As I always tell those who learn Cricut from my workshop, Cricut is much more than DIY projects, you can make money from the designs you make with the Cricut machine. You can also collaborate with other craftsmen to create wonderful designs. You can leverage on online groups on Facebook, and you can also get design inspiration from Pinterest for your next Cricut project. When it comes to Cricut, there is no limit to your creative ability, if you can think it, you can do it!

This book has taught you lessons on editing Cricut Projects, how to use the Cricut Design space on your Ipad, Android and Desktop. You have also learnt essential tips that will help you on your journey to become a Pro Cutter. Keep practicing and collaborating because that is the only way you can take your Cricut game to the next level and earn money from it. Check my other book on amazing Cricut Projects you can try in the "Other Books by the Author" section.

Made in the USA
Middletown, DE
27 December 2020